HEY! CHECK IT OUT!

Who What Where When Why?

Language Arts
SPELLING STINGERS...2
PARTS OF SPEECH...4
READING FOR DETAILS...6

Math
MULTIPLICATION MAGIC...8
THE AMAZING MATH MACHINE...10
TIME AND TEMPERATURE...12
BUILDING NUMBERS...14
MONEY MATTERS...16
FRACTIONS...18

Science
OUR SOLAR SYSTEM...20
BONES AND MUSCLES...22

Social Studies
GRAPHING SURVEYS...24
LANDFORMS...26

BACKGROUND MUSIC ON/OFF

Spelling Stingers

tonight	dime	name
moon	grade	balloon
adjective	skeleton	morning
hear	party	tear
sight	adverb	product
flame	house	muscle
spouse	nickel	time
quite	dear	quarter
Tuesday	fade	matter
latter	write	solar
comet	hour	maybe
sting	Earth	dollar
factor	Sunday	island
soon	been	plateau

FIND IT!

Word Families!

- •ime — chime, slime
- •atter — batter, splatter
- •ouse — blouse, mouse
- •ade — jade, spade
- •ear — spear, fear
- •ame — came, same
- •ite — bite, kite
- •our — sour, flour
- •oon — noon, spoon
- •ing — sing, bring
- •ight — fight, might

Parts of Speech

Noun — A noun names a person, place, animal or thing.

My **aunt** eats **bananas** in her **soup**.

Adjective — An adjective describes a noun. Some tell how many or what kind.

Silly Aunt Sally throws the peels to her **pretty** parakeets.

Action Verb — An action verb shows action. It tells what people or things do.

Aunt Sally's parakeets **peck** at the peels.

Adverb — An adverb tells about, or describes, a verb. Adverbs tell when, where or how.

The parakeets always sing **loudly** as Aunt Sally snoozes **downstairs**.

Pick A Part

Dear Sally,

I got a (ADJECTIVE) (NOUN) for my birthday, and (ADVERB) wanted to take it to school. My mom said no because I might (VERB) it. I snuck it in my (NOUN) without telling her. My friends and I played with it during recess, and I left it on the (NOUN) accidentally. I went back to school, but it wasn't there. I'm scared to (VERB) my mom. What should I do?

Sincerely,
Worried

camel	quietly	teacher	lumpy
eat	melt	suddenly	parrot
curly	pizza	spaceship	tickle
quickly	happily	grumpy	wildly
erase	clumsy	pillow	noisy
nose	square	jiggle	loudly
blue	carefully	yummy	frighten
gulp	paint	easily	tooth

LOONEY LETTER

Reading for Details

Spot, The Lazy Soccer Star Dog

Spot was one **exhausted** pup. Digging up daisies was hard work. All he wanted to do now was roll around in the grass, but Jeanie wouldn't let him. "Hey, Spot, stop that," she insisted. "We've got to practice your soccer trick for the Red Lightning's game tomorrow."

Spot hid his head beneath his paws. "Don't pretend you have a headache," warned Jeanie. "You're the star of the halftime show—and we don't want to **disappoint** your fans."

Spot **whimpered**. "Oh, dear, I forgot your dog biscuits," Jeanie groaned. "Please don't give me those sad puppy-dog eyes. I'll find something for you." Jeanie emptied her pockets.

"Look!" she exclaimed. "My red bandana! You can wear this at the game! You'll look **spectacular!**"

Spot jumped up and barked three times. "That's the spirit!" cheered Jeanie. "Now let's see you bounce the ball off your nose." Spot leapt into the air and sent the ball flying high above the Dogwood tree in Jeanie's front yard.

Jeanie laughed as Spot chased after the soccer ball. "You're heads and tails above all the other dogs, Spot!" Jeanie declared. "I think you're ready to play soccer!"

The 5 W's

Who are the characters?

What happened?

Where did it happen?

When did it happen?

Why did it happen?

It's in the details

1. What was the name of the Soccer team?
2. Where did Jeanie find a surprise for Spot?
3. How did Spot react to the red bandana?
4. What did Jeanie think of Spot's trick?
5. What bolded word means the same as "let down?"
6. What bolded word means the opposite of "dull?"
7. What bolded word means the same as "cried?"
8. What bolded word means the opposite of "full of energy?"

Multiplication

1s Trick

2s Trick

3s Trick

4s Trick

5s Trick

6s Trick

X	1	2	3	4	5	6
1	1	2	3	4	5	6
2	2	4	6	8	10	12
3	3	6	9	12	15	18
4	4	8	12	16	20	24
5	5	10	15	20	25	30
6	6	12	18	24	30	36
7	7	14	21	28	35	42
8	8	16	24	32	40	48
9	9	18	27	36	45	54
10	10	20	30	40	50	60
11	11	22	33	44	55	66
12	12	24	36	48	60	72

MATH TERMS

5x4 = 20

FACTOR   PRODUCT

Magic

7	8	9	10	11	12
7	8	9	10	11	12
14	16	18	20	22	24
21	24	27	30	33	36
28	32	36	40	44	48
35	40	45	50	55	60
42	48	54	60	66	72
49	56	63	70	77	84
56	64	72	80	88	96
63	72	81	90	99	108
70	80	90	100	110	120
77	88	99	110	121	132
84	96	108	120	132	144

7s Trick

8s Trick

9s Trick

10s Trick

11s Trick

12s Trick

Beat the Clock!

Magic Factor

Time & Temperature

half past four — quarter to two — twenty three past six
quarter past twelve — ten o'clock

1:45 10:00 6:23 12:15 4:30

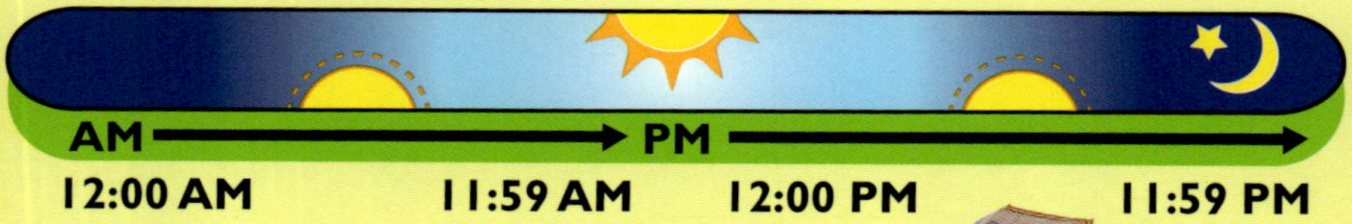

AM → 12:00 AM — 11:59 AM — PM → 12:00 PM — 11:59 PM

212°F
32°F

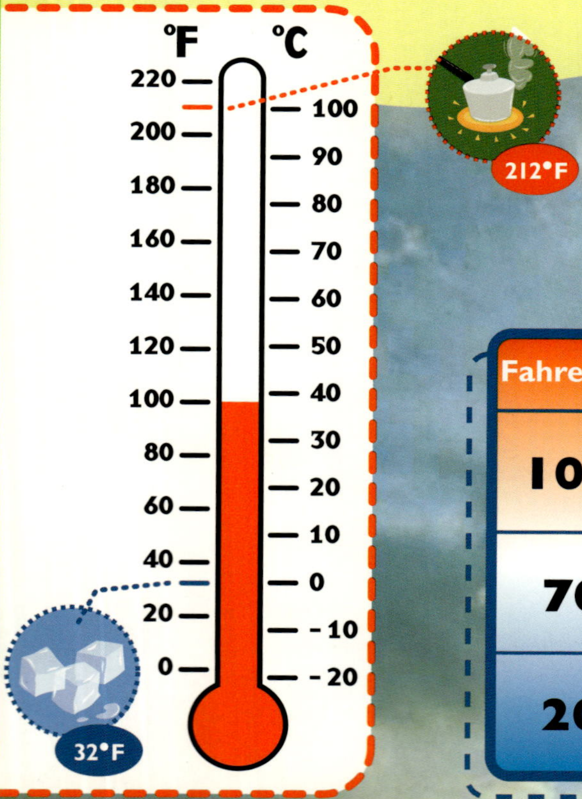

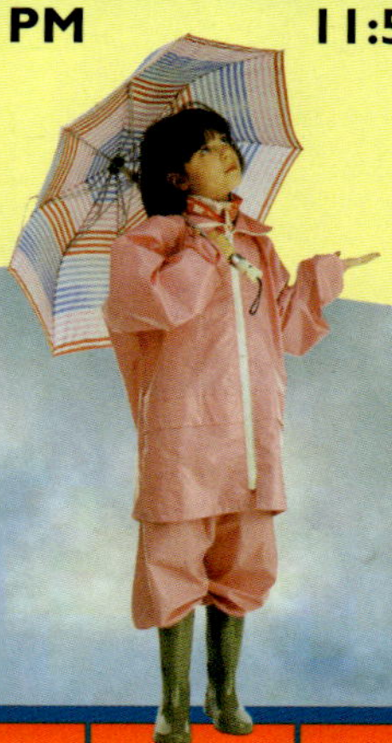

Fahrenheit	Celsius	Weather
100°	39°	Hot
70°	20°	Mild
20°	-7°	Cold

GO
STOP

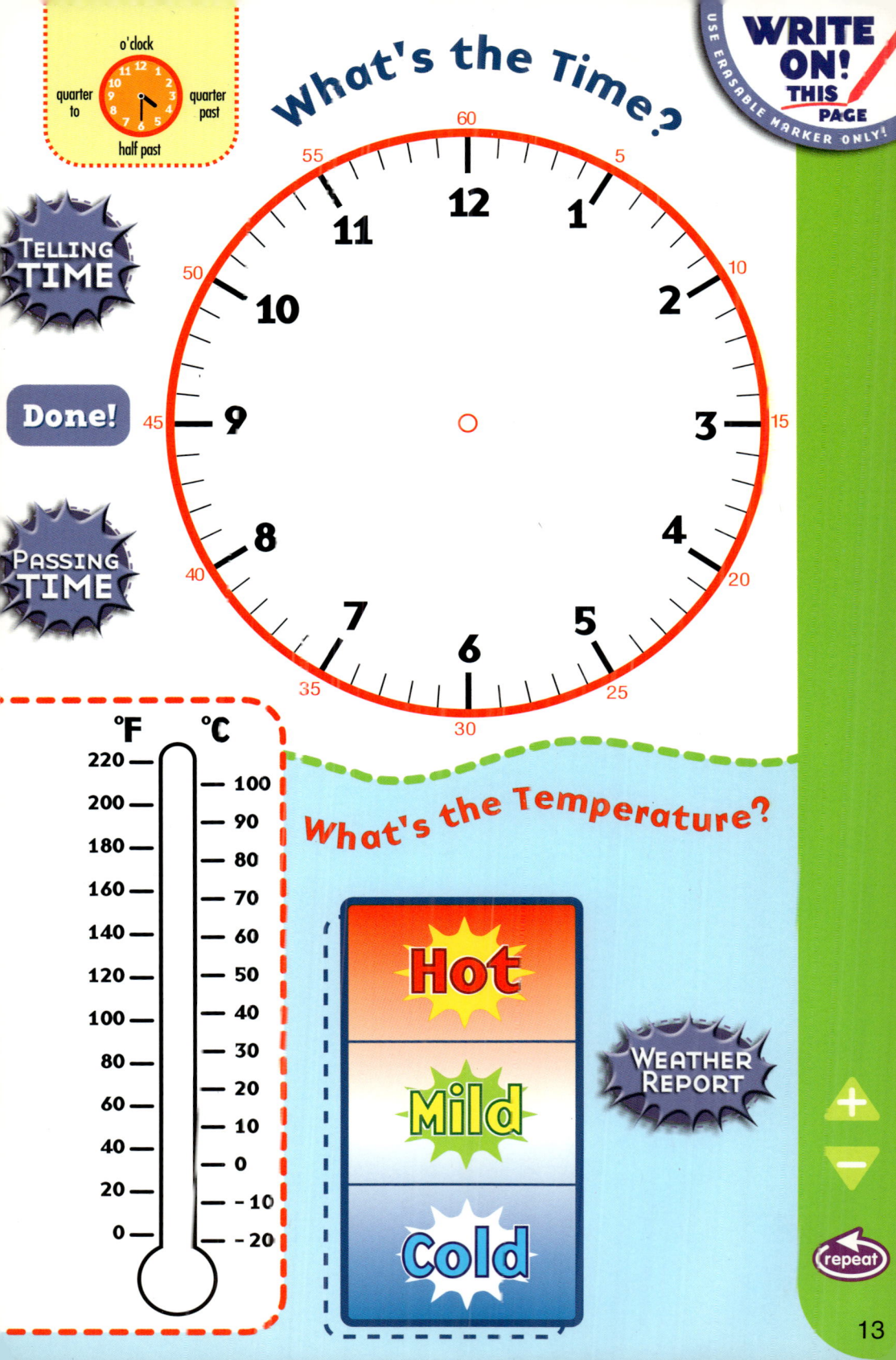

Building NUMBERS
Understanding Place Value

Hundred Thousands	Ten Thousands	Thousands	Hundreds	Tens	Ones

Standard Form

7 8 2 , 4 5 3

Expanded Form

7 0 0 , 0 0 0
+
8 0 , 0 0 0
+
2 , 0 0 0
+
4 0 0
+
5 0
+
3

562 2,040
8,920   74,085
27   479
18,654
400,373 7,769 53

Beat the Clock!

WRITE ON! THIS PAGE
USE ERASABLE MARKER ONLY!

Now You Try it!

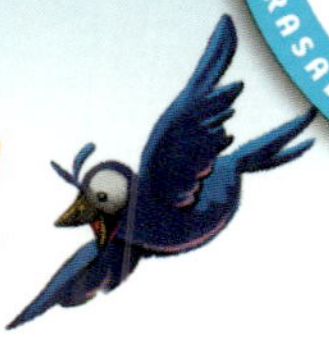

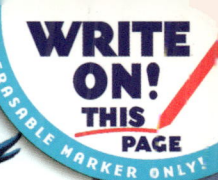

Hundred Thousands	Ten Thousands	Thousands	Hundreds	Tens	Ones

Standard Form

		,			

Expanded Form

		,			

+

	,			

+

,			

+

+

+

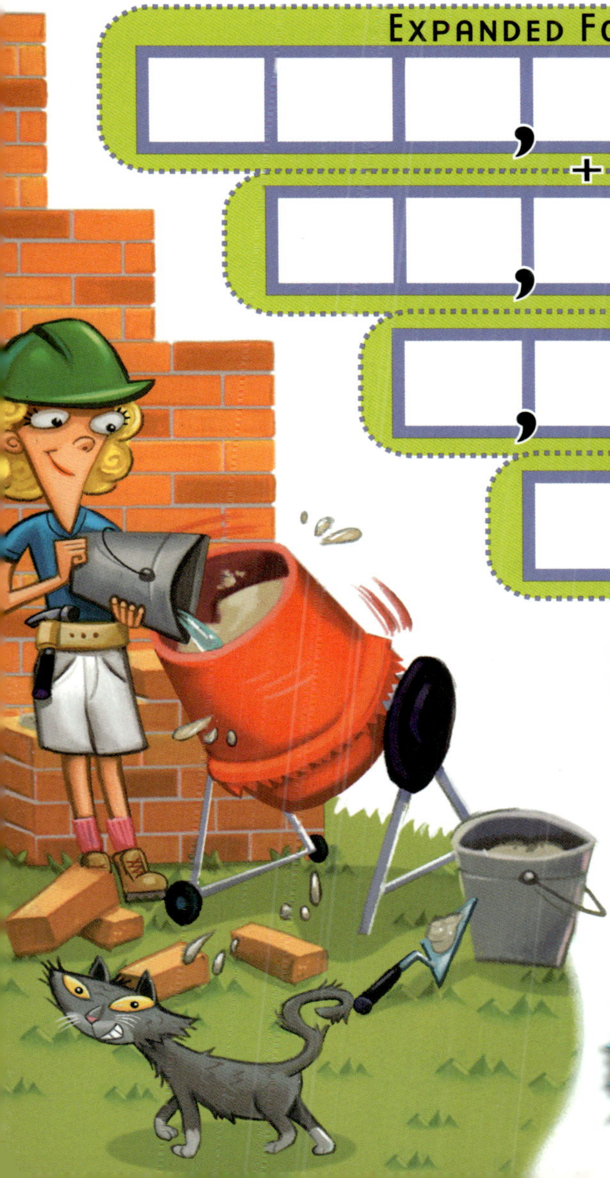

GO FOR IT!

Done!

repeat

Money Matters

Money Mystery

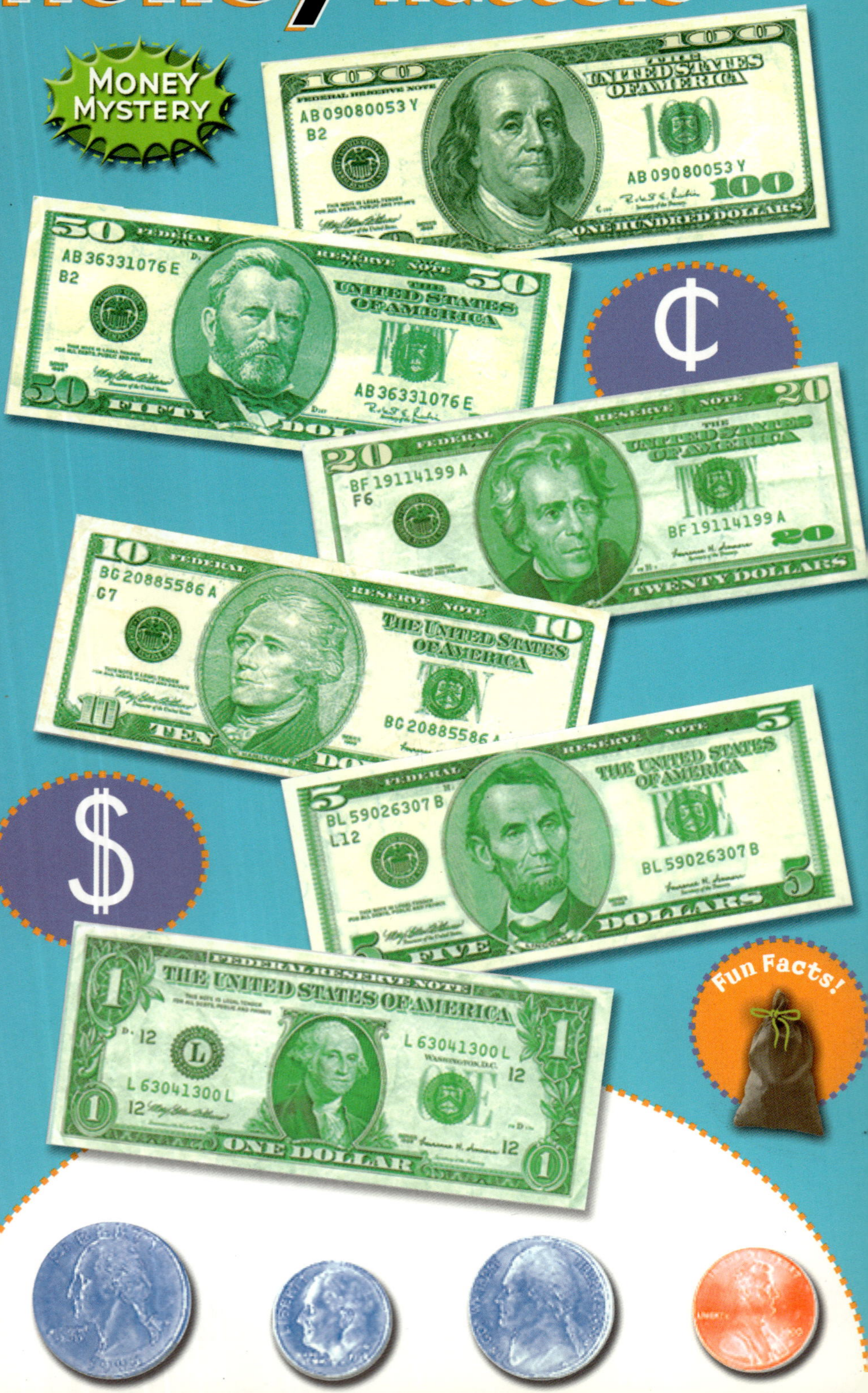

Fun Facts!

GO

STOP

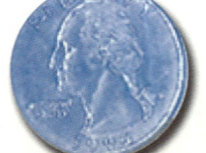

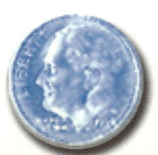

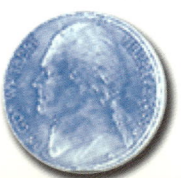

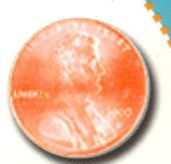

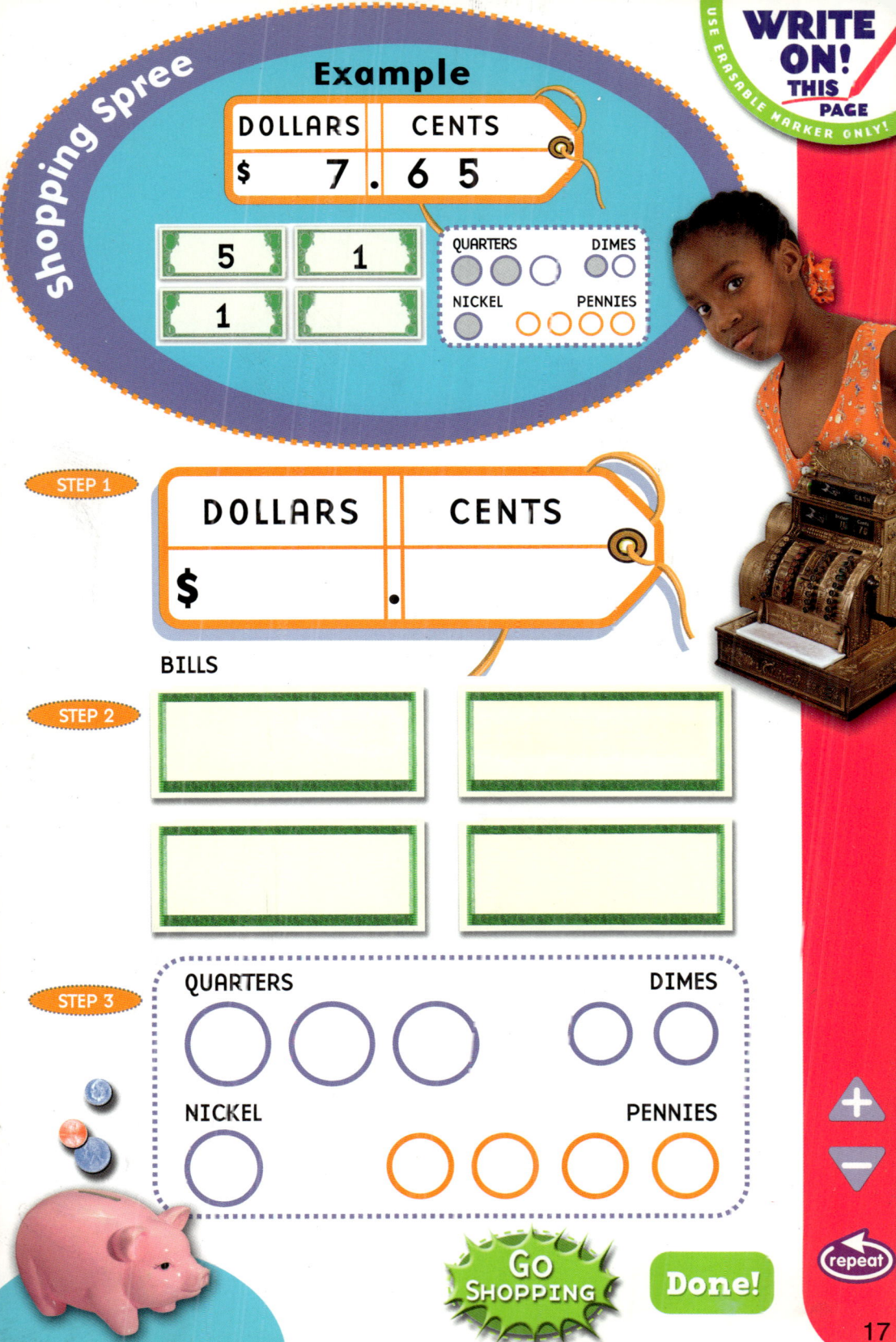

Fractions

Dividing a Whole into Equal Parts

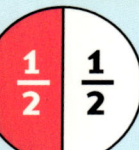
halves

thirds

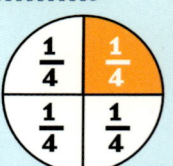
fourths

fifths

sixths

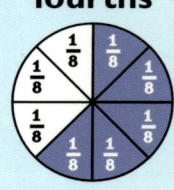
eighths

What's a Fraction?

$$\frac{1}{2} = \frac{\text{numerator}}{\text{denominator}} = \frac{\text{number of parts considered}}{\text{number of equal parts in the whole}}$$

Adding & Subtracting Fractions
with a common denominator

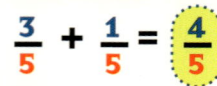

$$\frac{3}{5} + \frac{1}{5} = \frac{4}{5}$$ add numerators / use same denominators

$$\frac{3}{5} - \frac{1}{5} = \frac{2}{5}$$ subtract numerators / use same denominators

True   False

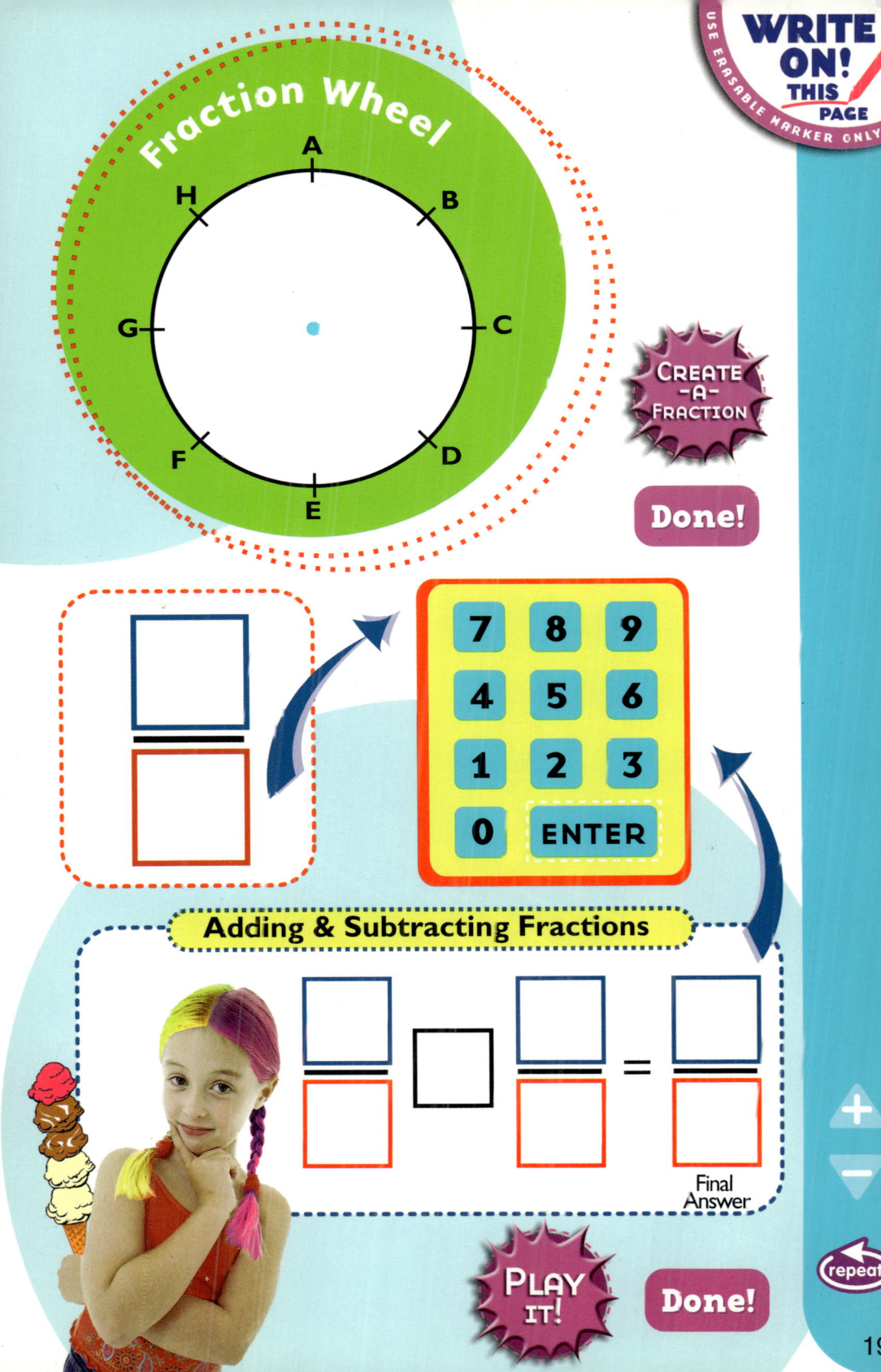

BONES and

Bones are made of living tissue and give your body shape. Bones also make new blood and protect your insides from harm.

1. cranium
2. mandible
3. clavicle
4. sternum
5. humerus
6. radius
7. ulna
8. ribs
9. vertebrae
10. pelvis
11. carpals
12. phalanges (upper & lower)
13. femur
14. patella
15. tibia
16. fibula

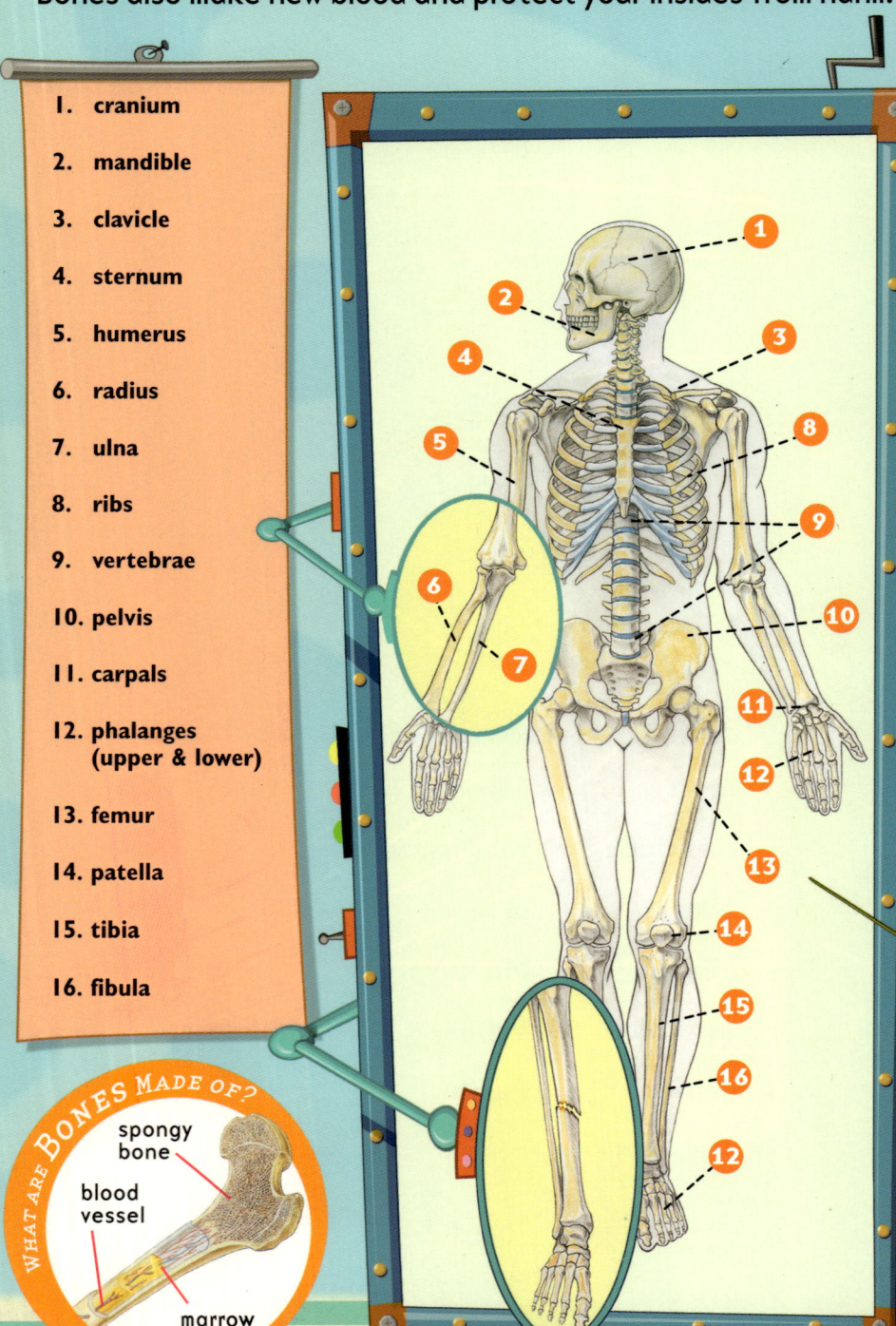

What are BONES made of?
- spongy bone
- blood vessel
- marrow

MUSCLES

Most muscles move bones, others move organs. The body has **voluntary** and **involuntary** muscles.

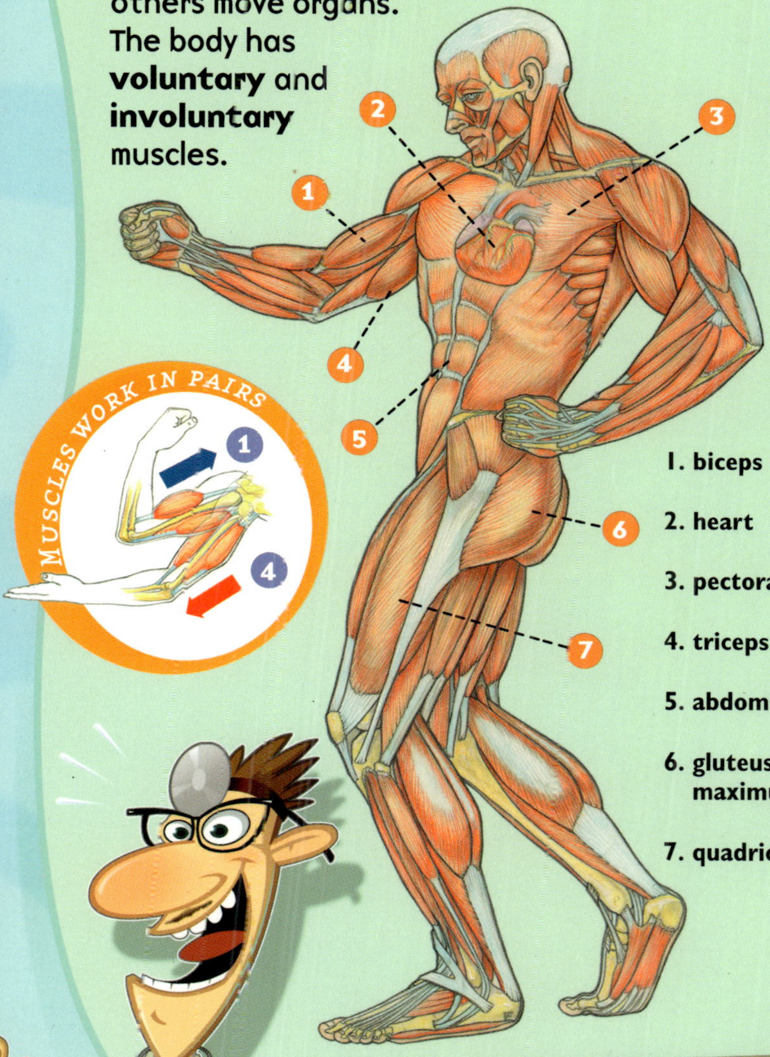

1
2
3
4
5
6
7
MUSCLES WORK IN PAIRS
1
4

1. biceps
2. heart
3. pectoralis
4. triceps
5. abdominals
6. gluteus maximus
7. quadriceps

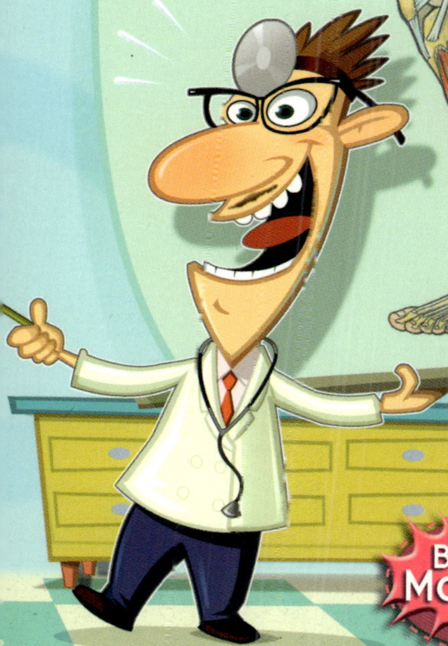

GO FOR IT!

BUILD A MONSTER

True

False

repeat

Graphing Surveys

Pictograph: Food

Pizza	🍕	🍕	🍕	🍕	🍕	🍕	🍕	🍕
Apples	🍎	🍎	🍎	🍎	🍎			
Broccoli	🥦	🥦						
Donuts	🍩	🍩	🍩	🍩	🍩	🍩	🍩	
Tacos	🌮	🌮	🌮	🌮				

Bar Graph: Sports

	Soccer	Baseball	Ice Skating	Skateboarding	Tennis
8	■				
7	■				
6	■			■	
5	■	■		■	
4	■	■		■	■
3	■	■		■	■
2	■	■	■	■	■
1	■	■	■	■	■

Graph-o-Matic

The Results Are In!

Food Findings

Done!

Pictograph: Food

Pizza	🍕	🍕	🍕	🍕	🍕	🍕	🍕	🍕	🍕
Apples	🍎	🍎	🍎	🍎	🍎	🍎	🍎	🍎	🍎
Broccoli	🥦	🥦	🥦	🥦	🥦	🥦	🥦	🥦	
Donuts	🍩	🍩	🍩	🍩	🍩	🍩	🍩	🍩	🍩
Tacos	🌮	🌮	🌮	🌮	🌮	🌮	🌮	🌮	

Bar Graph: Sports

8					
7					
6					
5					
4					
3					
2					
1					
	Soccer	Baseball	Ice Skating	Skateboarding	Tennis

Sports Spotlight

Landforms

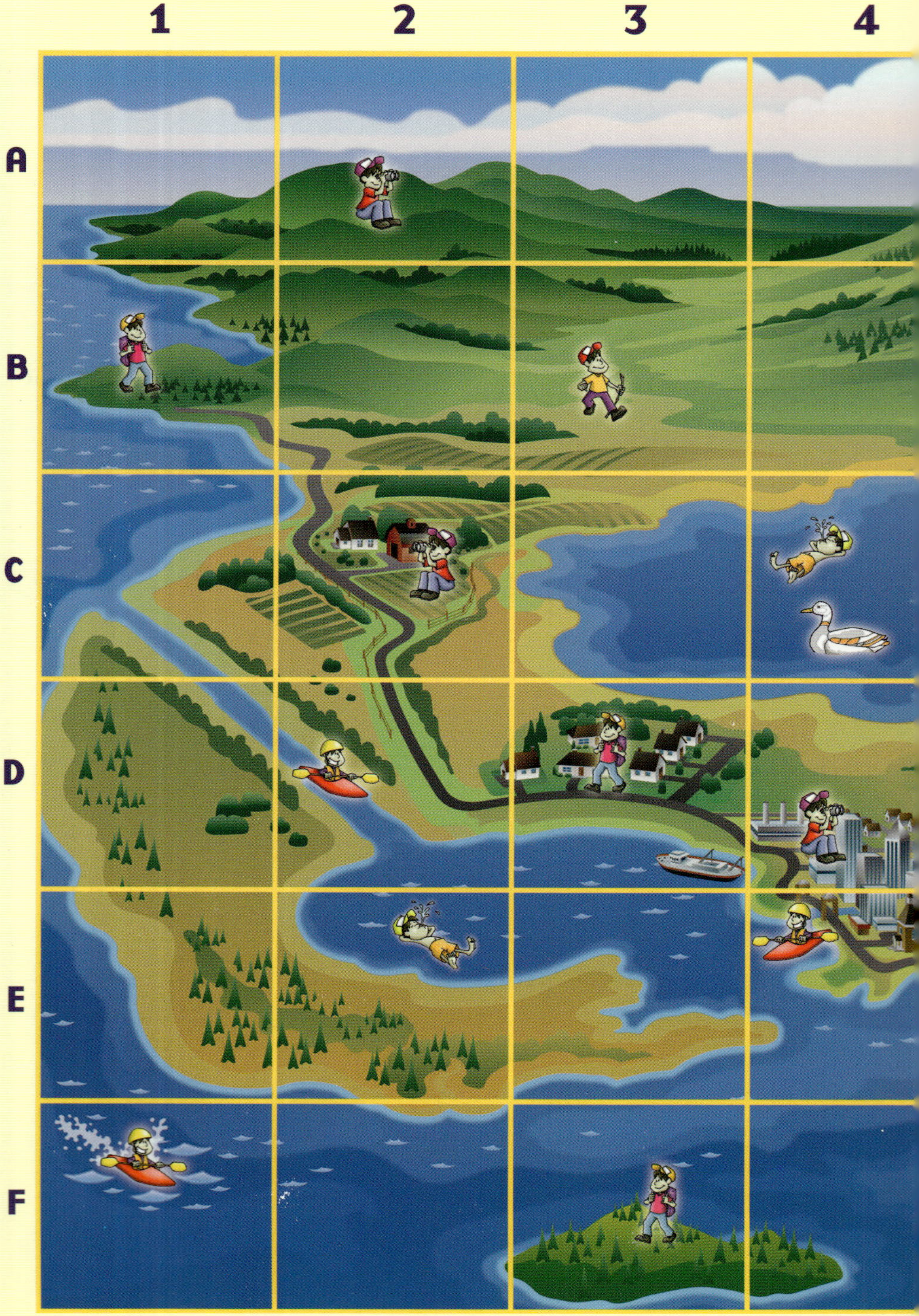

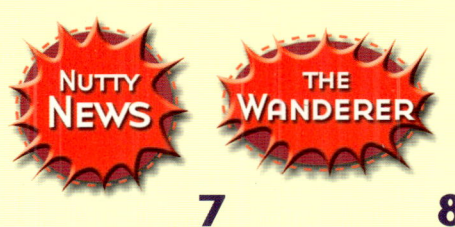

NUTTY NEWS

THE WANDERER

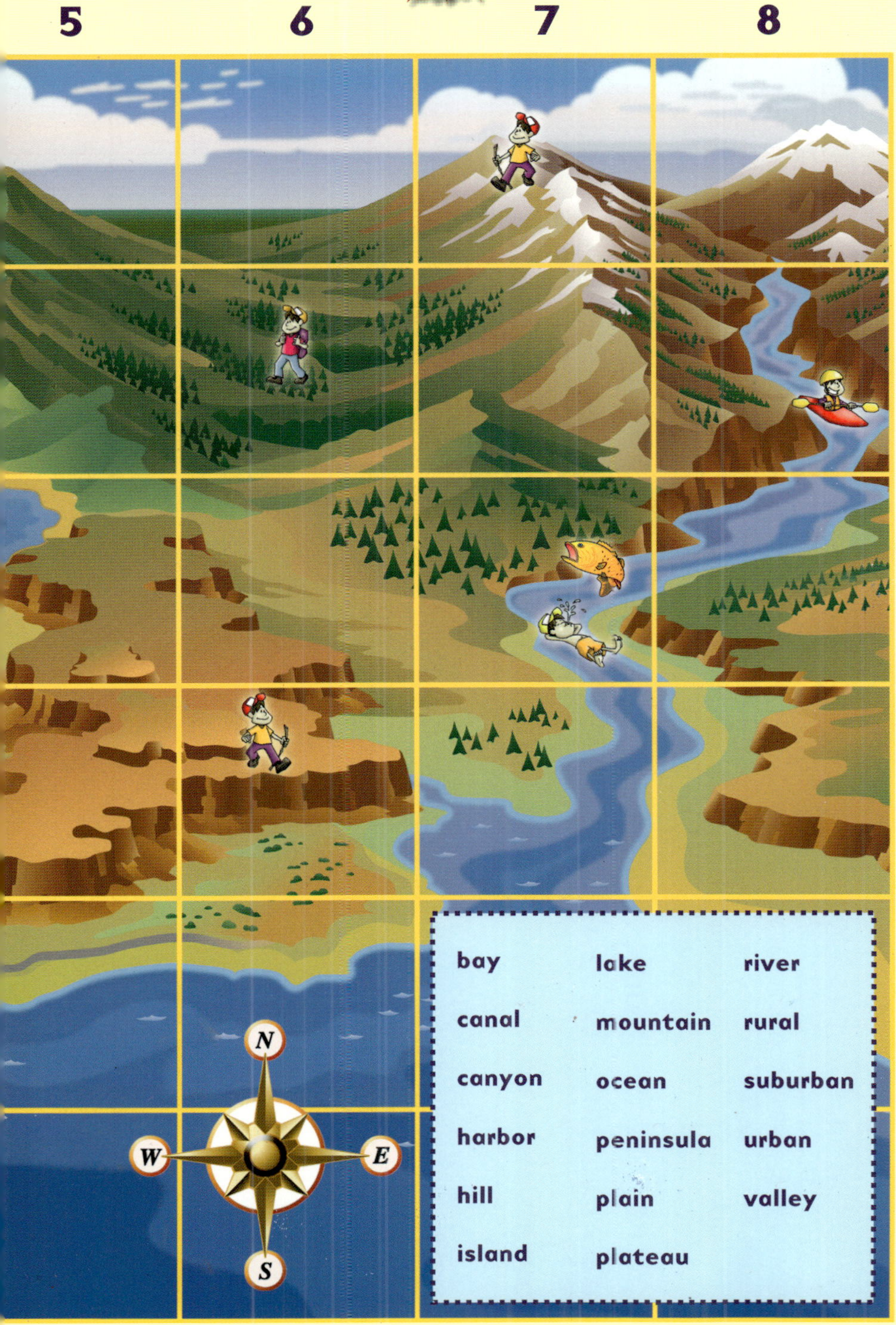
5
6
7
8
N
W
E
S
bay
lake
river
canal
mountain
rural
canyon
ocean
suburban
harbor
peninsula
urban
hill
plain
valley
island
plateau

+

−

repeat

Check out these fun products from Quantum Leap!

Whether it's the Spelling, Math, Vocabulator or the multi-subject BRAIN QUEST® edition, fast-action **Turbo Twist®** products are a fun way to reinforce what you are learning in school and help send you to the head of the class! New questions are downloadable from LeapFrog.com with a Mind Station connector. You can even create your own spelling list!

Explorer™ Globe is the interactive talking globe that lets you travel around the world, play exciting games, and learn amazing facts.

The **iQuest™** handheld is an interactive talking handheld that makes studying for tests fun with questions based on actual textbooks* for grades 5-8 in Math, Science, and Social Studies. Plus, it keeps you organized with a calendar, address book, notepad, dictionary, and calculator.

Learn Something New Every Day™!
Use the **Mind Station™** connector to download new activities from the Internet! You can use the Mind Station connector to expand Turbo Twist and iQuest handhelds.

* Not all textbooks included.

QuantumPad™ LEARNING SYSTEM

FUN-damentals™ SERIES

Smart Guide to 3rd Grade

MASTER FUNDAMENTAL SKILLS

Math
- Multiplication
- Division
- Time & Temperature
- Place Value
- Money
- Fractions

Language Arts
- Spelling
- Parts of Speech
- Reading Comprehension

Science
- Solar System
- The Human Body

Social Studies
- Graphing Surveys
- Landforms

Content Reflects State and National Educational Standards

3rd Grade Ages 8-9
An Interactive Guide to Fundamental 3rd Grade Subjects

GO

Smart Guide to 3rd Grade

Get ready to learn what you need to know in 3rd Grade!

How to use this book:

To start, insert the cartridge and turn on your Quantum Pad™ player.

GO Touch the GO circle with the attached pen every time you turn the page

STOP Stop audio and activity

Play a game

Volume control

repeat Repeat a question

Erasable marker

Quantum Pad attached pen

Write On!

WRITE ON! THIS PAGE USE ERASABLE MARKER ONLY!

Do!
1. Do use an erasable marker!
2. Do write your answers to the audio questions on Write On! pages (on the right).
3. Do use the marker eraser, tissue or soft cloth to erase your work.

DON'T!
1. Do NOT use permanent ink, pencil or crayon.
2. Do NOT use spray cleaner on this book. It may ruin the book and the platform.
3. Do NOT forget to erase your work.

STOP

Tip: If you accidentally use permanent marker, try writing over with erasable marker and then wiping off with a soft cloth. Sanford Expo 2® dry erase pens also work with Write On! surface. For Quantum Leap replacement pens, please contact us at 800-701-LEAP (5327).